Maps

If you need to know the way to go,

Get a map to tell you so.

The Classroom

- Window
- Bookshelves
- Teacher's desk and chair
- Shelves
- Table and Chairs
- Window
- Reading Center
- Writing Cent[er]
- Tables and chairs
- Act[ivity] Ce[nter]
- Science Center
- Door
- Shelves

A classroom map shows a plan of the floor,

Tables, shelves, windows, and doors. 5

6   **A city map shows buildings and streets,**

To help us find good places to meet.

A state map helps us find our way,

Cities, towns, and places to stay.

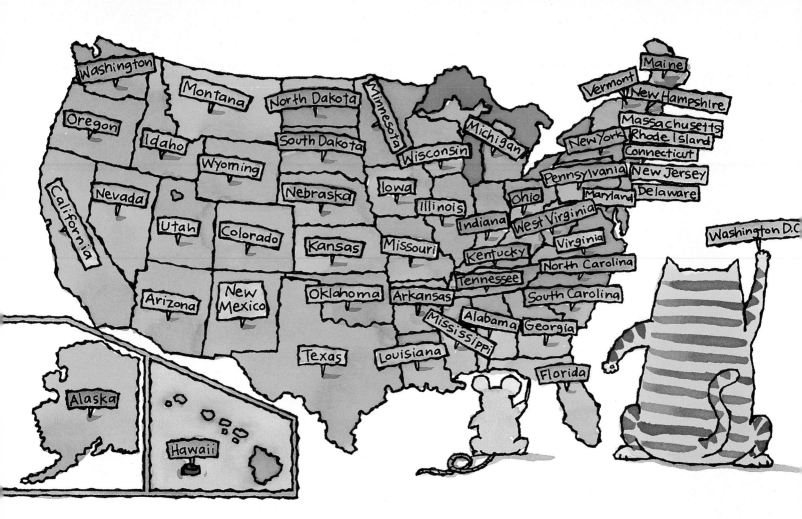

Our country's map shows every state,

Borders, cities, rivers, and lakes.

A world map shows us water and land,

Oceans, mountains, and desert sand.

If you need to know the way to go,

Get a map to tell you so!